'Do you see your son, standing over there, in the antechamber? Well, I am going to shoot him.'

D0718867

HERODOTUS
Born *c.* 484 BCE, Halicarnassus, Caria
Died *c.* 425 BCE, location unknown

This selection is taken from Tom Holland's translation of
The Histories, first published in 2013.

HERODOTUS IN PENGUIN CLASSICS
The Histories

HERODOTUS

The Madness of Cambyses

Translated by
Tom Holland

PENGUIN BOOKS

PENGUIN CLASSICS

Published by the Penguin Group
Penguin Books Ltd, 80 Strand, London WC2R ORL, England
Penguin Group (USA) Inc., 375 Hudson Street, New York, New York 10014, USA
Penguin Group (Canada), 90 Eglinton Avenue East, Suite 700, Toronto, Ontario,
Canada M4P 2Y3 (a division of Pearson Penguin Canada Inc.)
Penguin Ireland, 25 St Stephen's Green, Dublin 2, Ireland
(a division of Penguin Books Ltd)
Penguin Group (Australia), 707 Collins Street, Melbourne, Victoria 3008, Australia
(a division of Pearson Australia Group Pty Ltd)
Penguin Books India Pvt Ltd, 11 Community Centre, Panchsheel Park,
New Delhi – 110 017, India
Penguin Group (NZ), 67 Apollo Drive, Rosedale, Auckland 0632, New Zealand
(a division of Pearson New Zealand Ltd)
Penguin Books (South Africa) (Pty) Ltd, Block D, Rosebank Office Park,
181 Jan Smuts Avenue, Parktown North, Gauteng 2193, South Africa

Penguin Books Ltd, Registered Offices: 80 Strand, London WC2R ORL, England

www.penguin.com

This selection published in Penguin Classics 2015
001

Translation copyright © Tom Holland, 2013

Set in 9.5/13 pt Baskerville 10 Pro
Typeset by Jouve (UK), Milton Keynes
Printed in Great Britain by Clays Ltd, St Ives plc

A CIP catalogue record for this book is available from the British Library

ISBN: 978–0–141–39877–8

www.greenpenguin.co.uk

[1] This, then, was the Amasis against whom Cambyses, the son of Cyrus, was leading an army drawn from all the peoples subject to him, Greeks included – to be specific, Ionians and Aeolians. What lay behind the invasion? Cambyses had made a demand of Amasis, through a herald dispatched to Egypt, that he hand over one of his daughters to him – a demand which had in turn been made on the prompting of an Egyptian with a grudge against Amasis. This physician, alone among his colleagues, had been torn away by royal edict from his wife and children, and packed off to Persia, after Amasis had received a request from Cyrus for the best eye-doctor in Egypt. No wonder, then, that the Egyptian should have been so filled with resentment that he succeeded in pressing (indeed, almost instructing) Cambyses into asking for a daughter from Amasis – who was then confronted by the choice of surrendering his daughter at the cost of deep personal distress, or of rebuffing the request, and making an enemy of Cambyses. Already vexed by the menace of Persian power, Amasis found himself quite unable to answer yes or no. He knew full well that his

daughter would be taken by Cambyses not as a wife, but as a concubine; and so it was with this in mind that he finally settled on a course of action. It so happened that the one surviving member of the previous royal house was a daughter of Apries, a strikingly statuesque and handsome girl named Nitetis. Amasis duly arrayed her in fine clothes and gold jewellery, and sent her off to Persia, as though she were his own daughter. In due course, however, when Cambyses happened to address the girl by her father's name, she replied, 'You have no idea, my Lord, just how badly Amasis has abused you. Despite the fact that he dispatched me to you decked out in all this finery, as though it were indeed his own daughter that he had gift-wrapped, the truth is that I am the daughter of Apries, the one-time master of Amasis, but lately toppled and murdered by him, him and all the Egyptians.' Such was the declaration (and such the provocation that it served to bring to light) which led Cambyses, son of Cyrus, to descend upon Egypt in a towering fury. Or so, at any rate, the Persians report.

[2] The Egyptians, however, claim Cambyses as one of their own, asserting that he was the son of this same daughter of Apries, and that it was Cyrus, not Cambyses, who sent to Amasis for his daughter. In presenting this version of events, however, they are way off the mark. Indeed, since the Egyptians themselves have a better grasp than anyone of how Persian laws function, it can hardly have escaped their attention, firstly, that it is

wholly illegal for a bastard to inherit the Persian throne while there is still a legitimate heir alive, and secondly, that Cambyses was the child of Cassandane, the daughter of Pharnaspes, a man of Achaemenid stock, and not an Egyptian at all. The point of the distorted account given by the Egyptians, of course, is to provide them with a feigned link of kinship to the House of Cyrus.

[3] So that is how the matter stands. There is, however, another story – one that I personally do not find persuasive – which relates how a Persian woman came in to visit the wives of Cyrus, and was so impressed by the sight of Cassandane standing there with her tall and handsome offspring that she began to lavish extravagant praise on them. But Cassandane, who was one of Cyrus' wives, only retorted, 'Yes, and see with what a lack of respect Cyrus treats me, despite the fact that I have borne him such children. The only one he has any respect for is his new acquisition from Egypt.' These comments were prompted by Cassandane's resentment of Nitetis; and they were answered by her eldest child, Cambyses. 'That, Mother,' he told her, 'is why, once I am a man, I will turn all Egypt upon its head.' He was barely ten years old when he made this promise, to the great astonishment of the women. He never forgot it, however; and sure enough, no sooner had he come of age and taken possession of the throne, than he was embarking on his invasion of Egypt.

[4] There was another, quite distinct, episode, however, which also contributed to this expedition. One of the

mercenaries employed by Amasis was a man named Phanes, who originally came from Halicarnassus, and was both sound in judgement and bold in war. For some reason or other, he developed a grudge against Amasis, and fled Egypt by boat, his aim being to secure an audience with Cambyses. Such had been his standing among the mercenaries, however, and so detailed the intelligence he had on Egyptian affairs, that Amasis was frantic to capture him, and duly set about hunting him down. He dispatched in a trireme the most trustworthy of his eunuchs, who duly ran his quarry to ground in Lycia. Despite this success, the eunuch did not manage to transport him back to Egypt – for Phanes ran rings round his captor. First he got his guards roaringly drunk; then off he slipped to Persia. When he arrived, he found that Cambyses, despite his enthusiasm for leading his army against Egypt, was at a loss to know which approach to take, for none of the invasion routes offered any water, and so Phanes, in addition to the intelligence that he provided on Amasis, detailed the course that should be taken. 'Make contact with the king of the Arabians,' he advised. 'Ask him for safe passage.'

[5] Certainly, there is no other obvious way into Egypt. The territory between Phoenicia and the limits of the city of Cadytis belongs to Syrians who are known as 'Palestinians'; then from Cadytis (which I would estimate to be almost on the scale of Sardis), the coastal trading-posts as far as the city of Ienysus are subject to the Arabians;

beyond Ienysus, and all the way to the Serbonian marsh, where a spur of Mount Casium extends down to the sea, it reverts to Syrian control; onwards from the Serbonian marsh (in which some say Typhon lies hidden), and the crossing has been made into Egypt. The tract of land between the city of Ienysus and Mount Casium and the Serbonian marsh is no small distance, for it takes some three days to cross, and is so ferociously parched as to be quite without water.

[6] I am now going to point out something which few of those who make the voyage to Egypt have thought to reflect upon. Every year there is a constant flow into Egypt of earthenware jars filled with wine, imported from across the Greek world and from Phoenicia – and yet it is hardly an exaggeration to say that empty earthenware wine-jars are never seen. One might well ask, then, what on earth happens to them? This too I can answer. Every headman of a village is required to collect together all the earthenware from his own community and bring it to Memphis; and the people of Memphis must then fill the jars with water, and convey them to the same waterless stretches of Syria. This is the process by which every piece of earthenware imported into Egypt, once it has been emptied, finds its way to Syria to join all the other jars that have been assembled there over time.

[7] Now, it was the Persians, in the immediate wake of their conquest of Egypt, who provisioned the entry route into Egypt with supplies of water, in the manner I have

5

just described; but at the time, there was not a drop to be had. So it was that Cambyses, advised of this by his foreign friend from Halicarnassus, sent messengers with a request for safe passage to the king of the Arabians – who duly answered the pledges given him by granting pledges of his own.

[8] The Arabians, to a degree that few other peoples can match, regard the giving of pledges as a sacred business. Should two parties wish to make a compact, then the procedure is for a third man to stand between them and use a sharp piece of stone to score a light incision along the palms of their hands, just below their thumbs; he will then take a strip of cloth from both men's cloaks, and use the material to anoint with their blood seven stones which have been placed between them; as he does this, so will he invoke Dionysus and Urania. Once the ritual is completed, the man who is giving the pledge will commend the foreigner – or fellow-townsman, as the case may be – to his friends, and these friends will then regard it as their solemn duty to honour the pledge themselves. Apart from Urania, the only god whose existence the Arabians acknowledge is Dionysus; his cropped locks, they say, provide them with the inspiration for the way in which they wear their own hair short: that is, cut in a circle, with the temples shaved. Dionysus is called *Orotalt* by the Arabians, and Urania is *Alilat*.

[9] So it was that the king of the Arabians, after he had given his word to the messengers who had come from

Cambyses, devised the following plan. First he filled camel-skins with water and loaded them up onto every living camel he had; then, that done, he drove the camels out into the desert, and there awaited Cambyses' army. Such, at any rate, is the more convincing of the accounts that are given; but there is also a less convincing version which nevertheless, since it does have some plausibility, demands to be told. There is a large river in Arabia, the Corys by name, which flows into the Red Sea, as it is called. The story goes that the king of the Arabians had raw ox-hides and the skins of various other animals stitched together so as to make a pipe, sufficient in length to reach from this same river to the desert; and that he then channelled water through the pipe into large reservoirs which had been dug in the desert for the purpose of receiving and storing the water. It is twelve days' journey from the river to this particular desert. There were three pipes, and each one conducted the water to one of three locations.

[10] Psammenitus, the son of Amasis, made camp by what is known as the Pelusiac Mouth of the Nile, there to await Cambyses. Amasis himself was no longer alive by the time Cambyses came to invade Egypt, for he had died after a reign that had lasted forty-four years, and never once known any serious calamity. Following his death and mummification, Amasis was laid to rest in the burial-vault that he himself had had built within the shrine. During the reign of his son, Psammenitus, over

7

Herodotus

Egypt, a phenomenon was witnessed which utterly stupe-
fied the Egyptians: rain fell on Egyptian Thebes. This was
something that had never happened before; nor, according to the Thebans themselves, has it happened since, up
to my own lifetime. Rain is simply not a feature of upper
Egypt. On this one occasion, however, it did rain in
Thebes: a light drizzle.

[11] Once the Persians had crossed the desert, they took
up positions close to the Egyptians, aiming to engage
them in battle; whereupon the Greeks and the Carians,
who were employed as mercenaries by the Egyptian king,
felt so outraged by what Phanes had done in leading an
army of gibberish-spouting foreigners against Egypt, that
they devised their own riposte. Phanes had children
whom he had left behind in Egypt; and these children
were now brought to the camp, and into the full view of
their father. The mercenaries then set up a mixing-bowl
midway between their own and the enemy camp, after
which they led out the children one by one, and cut their
throats over the mixing-bowl. After the final dispatch of
all the children, wine and water were poured into the
bowl as well; the mercenaries then gulped down the
blood and headed off into battle. Fierce though the fighting was, however, and numerous the casualties on both
sides, it was the Egyptians who finally turned tail.

[12] I witnessed something truly extraordinary there,
which I was tipped off about by the locals. The site is
strewn with the bones of men from both sides who fell in

the battle, with those of the Persians quite distinct from those of the Egyptians, just as they were when the fighting originally began; and so brittle are the skulls of the Persians that, should you wish to make a hole in one, you would have only to tap it with a single pebble, whereas those of the Egyptians are so tough that it would be a challenge to smash them through, even if you pounded at them with a rock. Why should this be so? The locals gave a reason which seems to me eminently plausible: namely, that Egyptians are in the habit of shaving their heads from the very earliest days of their childhood, so that the bone ends up thickened by exposure to the sun. (This also explains why Egyptians never go bald – for it is a fact that the incidence of baldness among Egyptians is the lowest anywhere in the world.) This explanation of the toughness of Egyptian skulls also serves to suggest why Persian skulls should be so brittle: the Persians keep their heads out of the sun from birth by wearing conical felt caps, or *tiaras*. So that is how the matter stands. I saw something very similar at Papremis, when I inspected the skulls of those who had perished at the side of Achaemenes, the son of Darius, at the hands of Inaros the Libyan.

[13] When the Egyptians turned tail from the battlefield, they fled in disarray. Once they were all cornered in Memphis, Cambyses sent a Mytilenaean ship upriver, carrying a Persian herald whose mission it was to summon the Egyptians to negotiate. But the Egyptians, when they

saw that the ship had docked in Memphis, came pouring out from behind the fortress in a great mob; they destroyed the ship, butchered and dismembered the crew and carted the remains back inside the walls. They were duly put under siege and eventually brought to surrender. Meanwhile, the Libyans who bordered Egypt were so terrified by what had happened to their neighbour that they surrendered without so much as putting up a fight, accepted tributary status and started to send Cambyses gifts. So too did the people of Cyrene and Barca, whose alarm was no less than that of the Libyans. Although Cambyses looked smilingly upon the gifts he had received from the Libyans, he frowned upon those from the Cyrenaeans – because, I would guess, they were so meagre. All that the Cyrenaeans ever sent was 500 *minae* of silver – which Cambyses scooped up in his hands and tossed out among his troops.

[14] Nine days after taking possession of the fortress of Memphis, Cambyses installed Psammenitus, the king who had reigned over the Egyptians for six months, in the outskirts of the city, with the aim of testing him by offering him insult – Psammenitus and a group of other Egyptians too. First Cambyses had the daughter of the king dressed in the clothes of a slave; then he sent her out with a bucket to fetch water, together with other unmarried girls chosen from among the daughters of Egypt's most prominent men, and dressed in a manner similar to the princess. As the girls went past their fathers,

wailing and weeping, so all the other men, when they saw the humiliation inflicted on their children, wailed and wept in answer; but Psammenitus, the moment he had seen and fathomed what was happening, only bowed his head to the ground. Then Cambyses, once the girls with their water-buckets had gone by, sent out the king's son, together with two thousand other Egyptians of the same age, all of them with ropes tied around their necks and bits placed in their mouths. They were being led to the place where they were to pay the penalty for the massacre of the Mytilenaeans in Memphis, and the destruction of the ship, for it was the decree of the royal judges that, for every casualty that had been inflicted, ten Egyptians of the highest rank should die in return. But when Psammenitus saw the young men come out and pass him by, and learned that his son was being led to execution, he did not weep as all the other Egyptians who were sitting down around him did, nor betray any agony, but instead behaved exactly as he had done while watching his daughter. Once this procession too had gone by, it happened that one of his old dining companions, a man well advanced in years but who had fallen so far from his previous estate that he had been left with nothing more than a beggar might have, came asking for alms among the soldiers, and passed by Psammenitus, the son of Amasis, and all the other Egyptians who were sitting there on the city's outskirts. At the sight of this, Psammenitus let out a great wail of misery, and beat his head, and called to his comrade by name. Now there were men, it seems, who had been set to stand guard over him, and who had been keeping Cambyses informed about Psammenitus' response to all the various processions out of the city. His reactions astounded Cambyses; and so he sent a messenger to Psammenitus with a question. 'Psammenitus,' the messenger said, 'your master, the Lord Cambyses, wants to know why you neither cried out nor sobbed at the sight of your daughter being humiliated and your son going to his death, whereas a beggar who is not even a relation of yours, so he has been informed, solicited marks of respect from you.' To this question Psammenitus answered: 'Son of Cyrus, the evils that have afflicted my own household are too great to be wept over. Tears were, however, an appropriate response to the misery of my old companion, who on the very threshold of old age has been toppled from happiness and wealth, and come to beggary.' When these words were reported back by the messenger, they seemed to those who heard them well said. According to the Egyptians, tears rose to the eyes of Croesus (for he too, as luck would have it, had come to Egypt in Cambyses' train), and to the eyes of all the Persians who were gathered there, and even into Cambyses himself there entered some spark of compassion. And straight away, he gave orders that the son of Psammenitus should be spared the fate of all the other condemned men, and that Psammenitus himself should be raised up from where he had been sitting, out on the margins of the city, and brought into his presence.

[15] The men who had gone in pursuit of Psammenitus' son discovered that he had been the very first to be hacked down, and was therefore no longer alive; but Psammenitus himself was raised up and led into the presence of Cambyses. There he passed the rest of his days, and had to endure no further brutal treatment. Indeed, had he only had the good sense to avoid meddling, he would surely have had Egypt restored to him, and been appointed its governor, for it is the habitual policy of the Persians to honour the sons of kings, and even to hand back the rule of a kingdom to the sons of those kings who rebel against them. That it is their custom to do so can readily be deduced from a whole host of other examples. Particularly notable are the cases of Thannyras, the son of Inaros, who had the position of authority that his father had lost given back to him, and of Pausiris, the son of Amyrtaeus, who also had the rulership that his father had lost restored to him – and this despite the fact that there was no one who ever did more damage to the Persians than Inaros and Amyrtaeus. As it was, however, Psammenitus paid the price for all his plots and trouble-making: for he was caught red-handed inciting the Egyptians to rebellion. When all was made known to Cambyses, Psammenitus drank the blood of a bull, and promptly dropped down dead. That was the end of him.

[16] From Memphis, Cambyses proceeded to the city of Sais; he was minded to do something there that he did, sure enough, put into practice. No sooner had he arrived in the palace of Amasis than he gave orders that Amasis' corpse was to be exhumed from its resting place, and brought outside. Once this had been done, he commanded his men to whip it, to pluck out its hairs, to stab it and to inflict on it any number of other insults. The corpse, however, because it had been mummified, stood proof against all this and refused to fall to pieces, so once the efforts of his men had brought them to the point of exhaustion, Cambyses ordered the body to be burned. Such a command was sheer sacrilege, for fire is believed by the Persians to be a god. Indeed, the burning of corpses is contrary to the customs of both peoples: the Persians, following on from what I just said, claim that it is quite wrong to offer up a human corpse to a god, while the Egyptians hold fire to be a living, breathing beast, one that devours everything it gets in its clutches, until it is sated and expires after it has swallowed its final morsel. To give a corpse to any wild beast is absolutely contrary to Egyptian custom – which is why, to make certain that it will not be eaten by worms, they embalm it before laying it to rest. So the orders given by Cambyses broke the laws of both peoples alike. The Egyptians, though, claim that this outrage was inflicted not upon Amasis, but upon some other Egyptian of a similar age – and that it was actually this man whom the Persians were

insulting when they believed themselves to be insulting Amasis. The Egyptians say that Amasis had learned from an oracle what was fated to happen to him after death, and that in an effort to ward off what was coming, he had the man whose corpse had been whipped buried right by the doors inside his own tomb, and at the same time ordered his son to place his own corpse as deep as possible in the furthermost recesses of the tomb. It is my own opinion, however, that these supposed instructions of Amasis about how he and the other man were to be buried did not in fact originate with him but were made up by the Egyptians in an effort to save face.

[17] Cambyses' next step was to consult with his advisers on the viability of three separate military ventures: one against the Carthaginians, one against the Ammonians and one against the long-lived Ethiopians who inhabit Libya, beside the Southern Sea. Cambyses' decision was that he should dispatch his war-fleet against the Carthaginians, and a portion of his land-forces against the Ammonians; but that his first move against the Ethiopians should be a campaign of espionage. Under cover of taking gifts to the Ethiopian king, his spies were to reconnoitre all that they could, and in particular to find out whether the reports of Ethiopia's 'Table of the Sun' had any basis in fact.

[18] This Table of the Sun, the story goes, is a meadow situated on the edge of the city, filled with the roasted cuts of every kind of four-footed animal. All those who

happen to be serving as the city's officials at a given moment painstakingly deposit the meat there under cover of night; and then, come the day, whoever so wishes can go there and tuck in. The natives, however, say that the meat is generated every night by the earth itself. Such, then, are the claims made for the so-called 'Table of the Sun'.

[19] Cambyses' decision to deploy spies prompted him to issue an immediate summons to the city of Elephantine, to those men among the 'Fish-Eaters' who understood the Ethiopian language. His messengers went off to fetch them, and in the meantime Cambyses gave orders that all those in his war-fleet should set sail against Carthage. The Phoenicians, however, refused to do so: they declared themselves bound by the most solemn oaths, and that it would be the height of impiety for them to launch an assault against their own offspring. This reluctance of the Phoenicians to take part left the rest of the fleet quite inadequate to the task. So it was that the Carthaginians escaped being enslaved by the Persians. Cambyses, you see, did not feel himself justified in bringing force to bear on the Phoenicians, since they had freely submitted to the Persians, and because his entire war-fleet was dependent upon them. (The Cypriots had similarly submitted to the Persians of their own accord, and joined the expedition against Egypt.)

[20] Once the Fish-Eaters had arrived from Elephantine and come into the presence of Cambyses, he dispatched

them to the Ethiopians, complete with instructions as to what they were to say, and a whole load of gifts: a purple robe, a necklace of twisted gold, bracelets, an alabaster box of myrrh and a jar of palm wine. It is said that these Ethiopians to whom Cambyses was sending his messengers are the tallest and most handsome men in the world. Their customs are reported to be very different from those of other peoples; and none more so than the one which determines who becomes their king. The man in their city who is judged to be the tallest and strongest in proportion to his height – that is the man who is reckoned worthy of the throne.

[21] These, then, were the people visited by the Fish-Eaters, who duly handed over their gifts to the king, and said: 'Cambyses, the king of the Persians, desirous as he is of tying the knot of friendship and mutual hospitality with you, has sent us with orders to come here for talks, and to make a gift to you of these things in which he himself takes most delight.' But the Ethiopian could tell that they were spies; and told them so. 'You are nothing but liars, come here to spy on my realm! As for these gifts that you have been sent by the Persian King to bring me, they suggest no great desire on his part to establish links of friendship with me, but rather that he has no sense of what is right. How otherwise to explain this longing of his for lands that are not his own, and his hauling into slavery peoples that never did him any wrong? You are to give him this bow, and repeat these words to him:

"From the King of the Ethiopians to the King of the Persians, some advice. Only when the Persians can readily draw bows of an equal size should he think to lead an army against the long-lived Ethiopians – and even then, he should be sure to outnumber us. Meanwhile, let him feel proper gratitude to the gods that they have never turned the minds of the sons of Ethiopia to thoughts of adding other lands to their own." '

[22] And with these words, he unstrung the bow and handed it over to his visitors. Then he took the purple robe, and asked them what it was, and how it had been made. The Fish-Eaters gave him a truthful account of the purple-fish and the dyeing process; but the king only told the men that they were as deceitful as their garments. His second question was about the twisted gold necklace and the bracelets. The Fish-Eaters began to explain that the gold was for decoration; but the king, who thought that the bracelets were fetters, burst out laughing, and declared that the fetters in his own land were stronger by far. The third question was about the myrrh. The visitors described how it was manufactured and used to anoint the body; but the king dismissed it as he had similarly dismissed the robe. When he came to the wine, however, and learned how it was made, he had a drink and was delighted by it. 'What does your king eat,' he went on to ask, 'and what is the maximum span of a Persian man's life?' 'He eats bread,' they answered, and then explained to him how wheat is grown. 'As for the span of a man's life, the fullest

measure is set at eighty years.' To this, however, the king declared, 'I do not wonder that your lives should be so short, when all you eat is dung. Indeed, you would not even be able to stay alive for as long as you do, were it not for the restorative powers of this drink.' And so saying, he indicated the wine to the Fish-Eaters. 'For only in this do the Persians leave us trailing.'

[23] Then it was the turn of the Fish-Eaters to ask the king how long his own people lived, and what kind of things they ate. 'The majority', he answered, 'live to be one hundred and twenty, with some living even longer than that. As for our diet – we boil meat and drink milk.' When the spies expressed astonishment at the number of years, the king led them to a spring from which there came a scent like that of violets; and when the spies washed themselves in it, the water left them with a sheen, as though it had been olive oil. So delicate was this spring-water, the spies reported, that nothing could float on its surface: wood, and even things lighter than wood, just sank to the bottom. (Certainly, if the reports of this water are true, and assuming that the Ethiopians use it for everything, then it would indeed explain their longevity.) From the spring the spies were led to a dungeon full of men, where everyone was shackled with fetters of gold. (This because, among the Ethiopians, it is bronze which ranks as the rarest and most precious of metals.) Then, once they had seen the dungeon, they also saw the so-called 'Table of the Sun'.

[24] After this, and last of all, they saw the Ethiopians' coffins, which are said to be made of a translucent material. What the Ethiopians do with a corpse is to dry it out, either after the Egyptian manner or in some other way, and smear it all over with plaster and adorn it with paint, so as to render it as lifelike as possible; they then enclose it within a hollow column of translucent material (which they mine in great quantities, and which is easy to work). The corpse is now quite visible in the middle of the column, but without giving off any noxious stench, or indeed anything unpleasant at all. This column will be kept by the dead person's closest relatives in their home for a year, during which time they will bring him the first fruits of everything, and offer him up burnt sacrifice. Then, once the year has passed, they will carry it out and set it up among all the other columns which are dotted around the city.

[25] Once the spies had seen everything, they left for home. So angry did their report make Cambyses that he immediately launched an attack on the Ethiopians, without having built up any stockpiles of food, or taken into account that the target of his expedition lay at the very ends of the earth. Instead, mad as he was and quite out of his senses, he had no sooner heard from the Fish-Eaters than he went off with his army, the entire body of his land-forces, all except for the Greeks he had with him in Egypt, who were ordered to stay behind. Once the advance of his army had brought him to Thebes, he

ordered a detachment of his men, some fifty thousand in all, to bring him back the Ammonians as slaves and to burn down the oracle of Zeus, while he himself led the rest of his forces onwards against the Ethiopians. The army had not even gone a fifth of the way, however, before everything that they had by way of provisions was gone; nor did it take long, once the food had run out, for the pack-animals to disappear as well, for they too were all consumed. If, once he had grasped the situation, Cambyses had only revised his plan and led his army back, then he would have compensated for his original mistake, and shown himself a man of good sense; as it was, he took no account at all of what was happening but pressed on regardless. The soldiers, for as long as there was anything in the earth that could be scavenged, kept themselves alive by eating grass, but in due course, after they arrived in the sands, there were some of them who did a truly terrible thing: they cast lots, and devoured every tenth man among them. When Cambyses learned of this, such was his dread of cannibalism that he abandoned his expedition against the Ethiopians and went back; but by the time that he had returned to Thebes, he had lost a large part of his army. From Thebes he went downriver to Memphis, where he dismissed the Greeks and let them sail home.

[26] Such was the fate of the expedition against the Ethiopians. The invasion force sent against the Ammonians set out from Thebes, and was shown a route by guides

that indisputably saw it arrive in Oasis, a city inhabited by Samians who are said to belong to the Aeschrionian tribe, and who live seven days' travel away across the sand-dunes from Thebes. (The name of the place, in Greek, is 'The Isles of the Blessed'.) That the army made it as far as Oasis is a matter of record; but beyond Oasis we have no certain information about what happened to the Persians, since they failed to reach the Ammonians, and never made it home either. The only evidence derives, either directly or indirectly, from the Ammonians themselves, who have a story to tell. They claim that in the course of launching its attack against them across the desert from Oasis, the army arrived at a point approximately midway between them and Oasis; and as the Persians were taking their breakfast, a south wind of remarkable strength swept down upon them. Such a mass of sand was this wind carrying that when it deposited its load on the Persians, they were utterly engulfed – and so it was that they came to vanish. That, say the Ammonians, is what happened to the army.

[27] The arrival of Cambyses in Memphis coincided with the manifestation in Egypt of Apis, whom the Greeks call *Epaphus*. No sooner had he made his appearance than the Egyptians began to put on their finest clothes, and to hold street parties. When Cambyses saw what was going on, he jumped to the conclusion that they were celebrating his own failures, so he summoned the prefects of Memphis. Once they had all come into his presence,

he fixed them with a glare and asked them, 'Why, when the Egyptians never behaved in this manner the last time I was in Memphis, are they doing so now, after I have lost the greater part of my army?' The Egyptians explained that a god had appeared to them, and that because these appearances tended to be separated by lengthy intervals of time, it was the practice of all the Egyptians to celebrate each one with festivities. But Cambyses, having heard them out, told them that they were liars – and that he was condemning them to death.

[28] Once the executions had been carried out, he summoned into his presence the priests, who reiterated the earlier explanation. 'So some pet god has turned up in Egypt!' Cambyses exclaimed. 'Then I want to know all about it.' And with this declaration, he ordered the priests to bring him Apis, and they duly went off to fetch him. This Apis (or *Epaphus*) is a calf born of a cow which, from that moment on, evermore carries a barren womb. The Egyptians say that a beam of light descends from the sky onto this cow, and that it is from this light that Apis is born. The calf, which goes by the god's own name, has distinctive markings: although otherwise black, it has a white diamond upon its forehead and the likeness of an eagle upon its back, the hairs of its tail are double and it has a mark shaped like a beetle under its tongue.

[29] The priests brought in Apis, and Cambyses, who was teetering on the edge of madness, drew a dagger and struck at him, aiming for the belly but hitting the thigh

instead. Cambyses laughed, then spoke to the priests. 'You poor fools! What kind of god is born a thing like this, nothing but flesh and blood, and vulnerable to a touch of iron? The kind of god, no doubt, that you Egyptians deserve! But do not think you will get away with fooling me!' With these words he commanded those of his men who were responsible for such matters to flog the priests without mercy and to seize and kill any other Egyptians whom they found celebrating the festival. So it was that the Egyptians' festivities were broken up and the priests punished. Apis, struck in the thigh, wasted away where he lay in the shrine. Once he had died of his wound, the priests came and buried him without Cambyses knowing.

[30] The immediate consequence of this crime, the Egyptians claim, was that Cambyses went mad – although even before it he had barely been sane. The first victim of his criminal deeds was his brother Smerdis, who shared with Cambyses both parents, and who had already been packed off from Egypt to Persia. Smerdis had been the one Persian capable of drawing the bow brought back by the Fish-Eaters from the Ethiopian king, which he had pulled a distance equivalent to the length of two fingers, when none of the other Persians had managed even that. This had provoked Cambyses to much jealous resentment. Then, after Smerdis had left for Persia, Cambyses had a vision as he slept, in which it seemed to him that a messenger came from Persia, and reported to him that

Smerdis was sitting on the royal throne, and that his head was brushing the sky. This dream left Cambyses terrified that his brother might kill him, and rule in his place; and so off to Persia he sent Prexaspes, the man whom he trusted more than any other Persian, with orders to eliminate Smerdis. So Prexaspes went up to Susa, and killed him. Some say that he took Smerdis out hunting, and killed him then; others, that he led him down to the Red Sea, and drowned him.

[31] This, then, or so it is reported, was the first of the atrocities committed by Cambyses. His second victim was his sister, who had accompanied him to Egypt, and who not only shared with him both parents, but was his wife too: he had married her despite the fact that until then it had not remotely been the habit of the Persians to set up house with their sisters. It so happened, however, that Cambyses had passionately lusted after another of his sisters, and longed to marry her, despite the fact that what he had set his heart on was quite without precedent. So he had summoned the Royal Judges, as they are known, and asked them whether there might not be some law which obliged a man who wished to marry his sister to do so. (The men who become these Royal Judges are a select band of Persians; they remain in office until they die or else are convicted of some offence. They preside over all the cases brought by the Persians, and are the interpreters of their ancestral statutes: everything is referred to them.) The ruling they gave in response to Cambyses'

question satisfied justice without compromising their own security: they declared that, although they had failed to find a law which actually obliged a brother to marry his sister, they had discovered one which permitted the King of the Persians to do as he pleased. So it was that they avoided being intimidated by Cambyses into breaking the law, but not to the point of sacrificing themselves in its defence; for what they had found was a quite additional law, supportive of his desire to marry his sisters. The consequence was that Cambyses had married the one he particularly lusted after; but then, after barely any time at all, he had taken another sister as his wife too. It was the younger of these two sisters who had accompanied him to Egypt – and whom he killed.

[32] As with the death of Smerdis, so with hers – alternative stories are told. Greeks say that Cambyses threw a lion's cub into the ring with a young dog, and that this wife of his was one of those watching; the puppy was losing, but its brother [another young dog] managed to break free of its leash and came to its rescue, so that the one puppy became two, and the cub was duly vanquished. Cambyses was delighted by the show; but his wife wept as she sat beside him. When he noticed this, Cambyses asked her, 'Why are you crying?' 'I cried', she answered, 'because when I saw the puppy coming to the rescue of its brother, I was reminded of Smerdis, and it struck me that there is now no one to come to your assistance.' It was because of this comment, so Greeks say,

that Cambyses killed her. The Egyptian version is that one day, when everyone was sitting down around the table, Cambyses' wife took a lettuce and plucked off all its leaves, and then asked her husband whether the lettuce was more beautiful stripped bare or as it had been when still thick with leaves. 'When thick with leaves,' he said. 'And yet what have you done,' she answered, 'if not strip bare the House of Cyrus, so that it precisely resembles this lettuce?' So angered was Cambyses by this that he leapt on her; and she, who was carrying his child in her womb, suffered a miscarriage, and died.

[33] Such were the ways in which the House of Cambyses was affected by the madness brought on him by the business with Apis – or perhaps, bearing in mind how many ailments there are to which mankind is prone, his lunacy was caused by something else altogether. Indeed, it has been claimed that Cambyses was afflicted from birth by a particularly terrible ailment, called by some the 'sacred disease'. If so, it would hardly be surprising were a man afflicted by such a serious physical malady to be unsound of mind as well.

[34] His madness also affected other Persians. There is the story, for instance, of what he said to Prexaspes, a man whom he had always honoured above all others, appointing him court chamberlain, and his son as pourer of the royal wine – no small honour in itself. 'Prexaspes,' Cambyses is reported to have said, 'what kind of man do the Persians think I am? When they talk about me, what

do they say?' 'Master,' Prexaspes answered, 'they praise you to the skies, except when it comes to one thing – for they do say that you take your love of wine to excess.' Cambyses, thrown into a rage by this news of the Persians, answered, 'So now the Persians are saying that I am too fond of wine, are they? That it has driven me mad? That I am not in my right mind? Then what they told me before was just a lie!' He was alluding here to a previous occasion, when his Persian advisers, and Croesus too, were sitting in council with him, and Cambyses asked them how they rated him as a man, compared to his father. The Persians answered that he was better than his father, 'For you have everything that he had – but you have also won possession of Egypt and the sea.' That was what the Persians had to say; but Croesus, who was also present, judged this answer inadequate, and said to Cambyses, 'In my opinion, son of Cyrus, you are not alike to your father in all respects. This is because you do not yet have a son fit to compare with the son that he left behind in you.' Cambyses, who was delighted to hear this, lavished praise on Croesus' judgement.

[35] This, then, was the episode that he had called to mind. 'Find out for yourself', he raged at Prexaspes, 'whether what the Persians say about me is true, or whether it is they, when they report such things, who have lost their wits. Do you see your son, standing over there, in the antechamber? Well, I am going to shoot him. Now, if I manage to hit him directly in the heart, then that will

make it as clear as can be that the Persians have been talking nonsense. But should I miss him, then, yes, report as the truth what is claimed by the Persians, that I am indeed out of my mind!' So saying, he drew his bow to the full and shot the child – who fell to the ground. 'Cut the boy open,' Cambyses ordered, 'and identify where he was hit!' Then, when the arrow was found in the heart, Cambyses was put into such a good mood that he laughed, and said to the father of the child: 'You see, Prexaspes? It is as clear as clear can be. I am not mad! It is the Persians who have lost their wits! But tell me – have you ever seen anyone, anywhere in the world, hit the mark with a shot like that?' Prexaspes, seeing that the man was quite insane, and afraid for his own skin, answered him: 'Master, I doubt that even the god himself could have hit with such pin-point accuracy.' So much, then, for the behaviour of Cambyses on that occasion; on another, he apprehended twelve Persians who were equal in rank to the best, convicted them on some trifling charge and then buried them alive, head first.

[36] These actions prompted Croesus the Lydian to feel that it was his responsibility to have words with Cambyses. 'My Lord,' he said, 'rather than giving free rein to the passions of your youth, you should be keeping them under a tight control and getting a grip on yourself. Prudence is the best policy, just as forethought is the wisest. You are killing men who are your own fellow-citizens, executing them on the most paltry of charges, even killing

children! If you keep on indulging in such behaviour, watch out that the Persians do not rise in revolt against you. As for me, your father Cyrus repeatedly charged and instructed me to offer you criticism, and to recommend to you whatever course of action I should find the fittest.' Such was his advice; but Cambyses, despite the manifest goodwill with which it had been offered, replied: 'You have a nerve, to think to offer me advice! You – who governed your own country to such brilliant effect! You – who gave my father such excellent advice, when you told him to cross the River Araxes and attack the Massagetans, despite the fact that they were perfectly willing to make the crossing into our own territory! It was your incompetence when you were at the head of your native land which brought about your own downfall – just as it was the confidence that Cyrus put in your advice which brought about his. But do not expect to get away with it now! Indeed, I have been waiting a long time for an excuse to get my hands on you!' So saying, Cambyses grabbed a bow, intending to shoot him down; but Croesus leapt to his feet and ran from the room. Cambyses, frustrated in his attempt to use his bow, gave orders instead to his servants that they were to apprehend Croesus and put him to death. The servants, however, familiar with these swings in the royal mood, kept Croesus hidden; they reasoned that, were Cambyses to repent of what he had done and look to have Croesus back, they would be able to unveil him, and would be rewarded for having saved his life; whereas, if Cambyses did not change his mind, and did not come to miss Croesus, they could always finish off the job they had been given. In the event, Cambyses soon longed to have Croesus back, and the servants, once they had become aware of this, let the king know that he was still alive. Cambyses, however, though he acknowledged himself delighted at the survival of Croesus, declared that those responsible for it should not go unpunished, and sentenced them all to death. And put them to death is precisely what he did.

[37] There were many such acts of lunacy committed by Cambyses against the Persians and their allies; indeed, during his stay in Memphis, he broke into ancient tombs and examined the corpses. Similarly, he went so far as to enter the shrine of Hephaestus, and laughed uproariously at the image of the god. This statue of Hephaestus closely resembles the Phoenician *pataici*, which the Phoenicians carry around on the prows of their triremes. Should anyone never have seen one of these, it is best described, I think, as a likeness of a male pygmy. Cambyses also penetrated the shrine of the Cabiri, which only the priest may lawfully enter. There, he actually had the statues of the gods burned while pouring scorn on them. In appearance, these same statues are very similar to those of Hephaestus; indeed, the Cabiri are said to be his children.

[38] Everywhere you look, it seems to me, the evidence accumulates that Cambyses was utterly deranged, for why

otherwise would he have mocked what to others were hallowed customs? Just suppose that someone proposed to the entirety of mankind that a selection of the very best practices be made from the sum of human custom: each group of people, after carefully sifting through the customs of other peoples, would surely choose its own. Everyone believes his own customs to be far and away the best. From this, it follows that only a madman would think to jeer at such matters. Indeed, there is a huge amount of corroborating evidence to support the conclusion that this attitude to one's own native customs is universal. Take, for example, this story from the reign of Darius. He called together some Greeks who were present and asked them how much money they would wish to be paid to devour the corpses of their fathers – to which the Greeks replied that no amount of money would suffice for that. Next, Darius summoned some Indians called Callantians, who do eat their parents, and asked them in the presence of the Greeks (who were able to follow what was being said by means of an interpreter) how much money it would take to buy their consent to the cremation of their dead fathers – at which the Callantians cried out in horror and told him that his words were a desecration of silence. Such, then, is how custom operates; and how right Pindar is, it seems to me, when he declares in his poetry that 'Custom is the King of all'.

[39] At the same time as Cambyses was invading Egypt, the Lacedaemonians were launching their own campaign

against Samos, specifically against Polycrates, the son of
Aeaces, who had toppled the government there and taken
possession of the city. Initially, he had divided it up into
three, and given shares to his brothers, Pantagnotus and
Syloson; but subsequently, he had put the first of these
brothers to death, and driven the younger one, Syloson,
into exile, so that the whole of Samos became his. Having
done this, he tied the knot of friendship and mutual hospitality with Amasis, the king of Egypt, a pledge that the
two men sealed by the sending and receiving of gifts. And
straightaway, in next to no time, the affairs of Polycrates
had prospered to such a degree that they were being
bruited throughout Ionia, and across the Greek world.
No matter where he directed his campaigns, fortune con-
sistently favoured him. He built up a fleet of one hundred
penteconters and recruited a thousand archers, raiding
and plundering without discrimination – indeed, he used
to say that he would earn more gratitude from friends by
restoring to them what he had taken from them than he
would have done by not taking it in the first place. Many
were the islands he conquered, and numerous the cities
on the mainland too. Among his victories was the defeat
that he inflicted at sea upon the men of Lesbos, who had
sent their entire force to the assistance of the Milesians, but
now became his prisoners; labouring in chains, they dug
the whole of the moat which encircles the walls of Samos.

[40] Now, as may well be imagined, Polycrates' astounding good fortune did not go unnoticed by Amasis, who

was unsettled by it. Eventually, with Polycrates' run of luck continuing to bring him ever greater successes, Amasis wrote a letter and sent it off to Samos. 'Here is what Amasis has to say to Polycrates,' it read. 'How pleasant it is to learn that a friend, a man who is bound to one by ties of mutual hospitality, is faring so well. Nevertheless, your astounding good fortune is not a cause of unconfined joy to me – for I well know that the gods are given to envy. What I wish for myself, and for those I care about – if I may put it like this – is a career that blends good fortune with the occasional stumble. Better to go through life experiencing bad as well as good luck than to know nothing but success. I have never yet known nor heard tell of anyone who enjoyed a prosperity so total that he did not ultimately come to a bad end and lose everything that had previously sustained him. That being so, I would advise you, in the face of all your good fortune, to adopt the following policy. Think hard, and identify the object that is most precious to you, the one that it would cause you the most heartache to lose – and then throw it away, some place where there is no chance of its ever coming back into human hands. If, by the time you get to read this, there have still been no disasters to punctuate your run of good fortune, then remedy the situation in the manner that I have here suggested.'

[41] Once Polycrates had read this through, and after reflection had come to appreciate that the advice offered him by Amasis made good sense, he sought to identify

which of his treasures it would most pain him to lose. After much soul-searching, he fixed upon the signet-ring that he habitually wore: its stone, an emerald, was set in gold, and had been worked by Theodorus, the son of Telecles, a Samian. Accordingly, once he had decided that this was the treasure he would throw away, what Polycrates did was to man a penteconter, board it and order it out to the open sea. Next, with the island left far behind, he took off his signet-ring and threw it into the sea, in the full view of everyone on board. Then, that once done, he sailed back to Samos, where he retired to his home and mourned his loss.

[42] It so happened, however, five or six days after this, that a fisherman caught a large and beautiful fish, and thought it only fitting to make a gift of it to Polycrates. He hauled it to the front doors, where he announced that he wished to come into the sight of Polycrates. Permission was granted and the fish handed over. 'My king,' the fisherman said, 'although I am a man who has no living aside from what I catch with my own hands, I knew, when I caught this one, that it would be quite wrong for me to take it to the market-square. Such a fish, it struck me, is really worthy only of you and of your administration – which is why I have brought it here and given it to you.' Polycrates, who was delighted by these words, answered him: 'And excellently well done it is too! I owe you a double debt of gratitude – both for what you have said and for what you have given me. We invite you to come

35

and dine with us this evening.' The fisherman went back home bursting with pride; but the servants, when they sliced open the fish, found in its stomach the very signet-ring of Polycrates! No sooner had they laid their eyes on it and taken it out than they were carrying it into the presence of Polycrates in a state of high excitement; and as they presented him with the signet-ring, they told him how it had been found. And at this, there came into Polycrates' mind a sense of how touched by the numinous the whole business surely was; so he wrote down in a letter a full account of what he had done and what had happened, and then, when he had finished writing, sent it off to Egypt.

[43] When Amasis read the letter that had come from Polycrates, he realized that it was quite impossible for one man to redeem another from something that is inevitably going to happen, and that Polycrates, a man touched by such unfailing good fortune that even those things he threw away were found again, was certainly not someone destined for a happy end. So Amasis sent a herald to Samos with news that the treaty of mutual friendship between them was dissolved. His motive for doing this was to ensure that when some great and terrible calamity did eventually befall Polycrates, he would not feel in his heart the pain that he would feel for a man who was his friend.

[44] It was against this same Polycrates, the one whose luck knew no bounds, that the Lacedaemonians launched

a military offensive, in answer to an appeal from a faction on Samos that would later go on to found Cydonia in Crete. Now, at the time when Cambyses, the son of Cyrus, had been assembling his army for the invasion of Egypt, Polycrates, going behind the Samians' backs, had sent him a herald. 'Send me a request for troops,' Polycrates had requested, 'back here in Samos.' Cambyses, once he had listened to this message, was more than happy to send a message of his own back to Samos, asking Polycrates to dispatch a naval task-force to help him take on Egypt. The townsmen duly nominated by Polycrates, all of whom were on his list of likely subversives, were sent off in forty warships, together with instructions to Cambyses never to send them back.

[45] There are some who say that these Samians packed off by Polycrates never actually made it to Egypt, but only sailed as far as the waters off Carpathos, where they held a council of war and decided that they did not want to continue any further with their voyage. Others claim that they did make it to Egypt, where they were interned, but managed to slip away. Then, as were making their voyage back to Samos, Polycrates came out to meet them with his fleet, and engaged them in a battle – which was won by the returning exiles. When they landed on the island, however, they had the worst of an infantry battle and this is why they sailed to Lacedaemon. Yet others, however, claim that the Samians who had come back from Egypt did in fact beat Polycrates – a story which seems

most implausible to me. Why, after all, would they have needed to ask the Lacedaemonians for assistance if they were capable of overthrowing Polycrates on their own? What is more, it goes against all logic to imagine that a man backed up by hired auxiliaries and a vast squad of archers, recruited from among his own people, could conceivably have been defeated by the few returning Samians. As a safeguard, Polycrates also crammed the wives and children of his subjects into the ship-sheds, ready to set fire to them, ship-sheds and all, should his fellow-townsmen decide to desert to the returning exiles.

[46] When the Samians who had been expelled by Polycrates arrived in Sparta, they came into the presence of the authorities, and spoke at great length, commensurate with their need. The response of the authorities to this first audience, however, was to complain that they could not remember the early section of the speech, and had failed to understand what came after. As a consequence, when the Samians gained a second audience, they simply came in with a sack and said nothing at all, except to comment, 'This sack needs barley-meal.' 'There was no need to say "sack",' came back the reply. The Lacedaemonians resolved, nevertheless, that they would indeed give aid.

[47] So they made their preparations for the campaign against Samos and set off. They did this, according to the Samians, because they owed a debt of gratitude for the naval assistance that the Samians had provided some time

previously in their war against the Messenians; but the Lacedaemonians themselves say that they were prompted to launch their campaign less out of any desire to assist the Samians in their hour of need than because they wished to be avenged for the theft of the mixing-bowl which they had been taking to Croesus, and of a breast-plate which Amasis, the king of Egypt, had sent them as a gift. It is certainly the case that a year before they stole the bowl the Samians had indeed carried off this same breastplate, which was made of linen, had a large number of figures woven into it and was embroidered with gold and cotton. Most wondrous of all, however, is that each one of the breastplate's threads, fine though it is, consists in turn of three hundred and sixty separate threads, all of them clear to the eye. There is another breastplate, exactly like it, which Amasis presented as an offering to Athena in Lindus.

[48] The Corinthians, because they wished to ensure that the campaign against Samos did go ahead, had enthusiastically joined in: they too, a generation previously, at around the same time as the bowl was stolen, had been grievously insulted by the Samians. Three hundred boys, the sons of the leading men of Corcyra, had been sent by Periander, the son of Cypselus, to Alyattes in Sardis to be castrated. The Corinthians who were escorting the boys put in at Samos; when the whole story came out, and the Samians discovered why the boys were being taken to Sardis, their first step was to instruct the

boys to take sanctuary in the shrine of Artemis; next, they refused to turn a blind eye to the attempts that were being made to drag the suppliants away from the sanctuary; and then, when the Corinthians blocked the boys' food supply, the Samians instituted a festival which they still celebrate to this day just as it was first established. Every nightfall, for the entire time spent by the boys in the sanctuary, the Samians so arranged things that unmarried girls and boys would stage dances; and next, having arranged these dances, they made it a rule that the dancers should carry cakes of sesame and honey, which could then be snatched by the sons of the Corcyrans to provide them with sustenance. This continued until the Corinthians who had been guarding the boys gave up and went away – at which point the Samians took the boys back to Corcyra.

[49] Now had the Corinthians and the Corcyrans been on good terms with one another after Periander died, such an episode would hardly have provided the Corinthians with sufficient motivation to join the campaign. As it was, however, despite their shared kinship, the two peoples had been at odds with one another ever since the first colonization of the island. No wonder, then, that the Corinthians should have kept the wrong done them by the Samians very much in their minds. It was Periander's desire for vengeance that had prompted him to nominate the sons of the leading men of Corcyra for castration, and then to send them to Sardis, for the Corcyrans, by

committing an atrocious crime against him, had been the ones who first began the feud.

[50] It so happened, after Periander had killed his wife Melissa, that a very similar misfortune came hard on the heels of the one that had already befallen him. Melissa had borne him two sons: one of them now seventeen and the other eighteen years old. They were sent for by Procles, the tyrant of Epidaurus, who was their maternal grandfather, and who treated them with great kindness – as was only to be expected, of course, since they were the sons of his daughter. But when Procles came to send them back, he said, as they parted from him, 'Do you know, my boys, who it was killed your mother?' This was a question to which the elder of the two paid not the slightest attention, but which Lycophron, as the younger was called, found so painful to hear that he refused, on his arrival in Corinth, to engage his father – as the murderer of his mother – in conversation; not only that, but he refused to respond to any of Periander's attempts to talk to him, or to ask him questions. Eventually, Periander became so infuriated that he threw Lycophron out of his house.

[51] Then, once he had driven his younger son away, he asked the older one what the father of their mother had said to them. 'He received us with great kindness,' the son answered, 'but as for his parting words, they have quite slipped my mind. No, I cannot recall them.' Periander, however, persisted with his questioning, arguing

that Procles was very unlikely to have made no suggestion
to them at all; and then the boy did recall what Procles
had said, and repeated it. So it was that Periander grasped
what had happened; and, determined not to be swayed
by sentiment, he sent a messenger to the people with
whom his exiled son had made a new life, and ordered
them not to take him in any longer. And so it went on:
Lycophron would no sooner find somewhere to stay after
he was expelled than he would be kicked out of his new
home as well, since all those who opened their doors to
him would receive threats from Periander and orders to
send him packing. And every time Lycophron was sent
packing, he would go to another of his comrades; and
they, despite being terrified, would let him in, on the
grounds that he was, after all, the son of Periander.

[52] In the end, Periander issued a proclamation,
declaring that a fine payable to Apollo, holy in character
and set by him at a specific rate, would be imposed upon
anyone who might offer shelter to Lycophron or engage
him in conversation. Sure enough, as a consequence of
this edict, there was no one willing to speak to the boy
or to offer him hospitality. Even Lycophron himself
thought it wrong to try to defy the prohibitions, and
instead, because he still refused to back down, he just
hung around the colonnades instead. Three days passed,
and on the fourth, seeing how filthy and emaciated his
son was, Periander felt such pity that he stifled his anger
and approached him. 'My boy,' he said, 'which of these

two states is preferable – the one that you are currently in, or the condition of power and plenty that is mine, and which it is yours to inherit if you will only pay the respect that is due your father? You are my son, a prince of this rich and happy city of Corinth – and yet you choose to lead the life of a wandering beggar, and make me, the man who least deserves such treatment, the object of all your hostility and rage. Remember that if something terrible has happened to make you suspicious of me, then I too am caught up in the same business. More so, indeed, than you – for it was I who actually committed the deed. You have learned two lessons both at once: how much better it is to be envied than to be pitied, and what it means to indulge oneself in anger against one's parent and superior. Come, then, return home.' Such was the attempt made by Periander to win back his son; but the only answer that Lycophron gave was to say, 'You owe the god a fine for having come into conversation with me.' It was now that Periander appreciated just how far gone his son was, and how impregnable his condition of misery; so he sent him out of sight by having him shipped off to Corcyra (which was also then subject to Periander's rule). Next, with Lycophron sent on his way, Periander led an army against the man whom he blamed more than any other for what had happened to him: Procles, his father-in-law. Epidaurus fell, and Procles too, who was taken alive.

[53] Time passed, and as Periander grew older, he was

brought to acknowledge that his ability to oversee and manage the affairs of state was no longer what it had been. Accordingly, unable to distinguish any mark of talent in his elder son, who struck him as manifestly lacking in intelligence, Periander sent to Corcyra, summoning Lycophron to take up the reins of supreme power. Even when Lycophron disdained to give the bearer of this message an answer, Periander would still not relinquish his hopes of the young man, but instead, as a second messenger, sent the person whom he calculated would prove more liable to persuade his son than anyone else: his own daughter, the sister of Lycophron. 'Silly boy,' the girl said, on her arrival, 'do you really want supreme power falling into the hands of others? Your patrimony plundered? Would you really rather that than return and have it for yourself? Get back home with you now and stop putting yourself through this torture! Pride is a thing that cripples a man, just as two wrongs do not make a right! Plenty have put pragmatism ahead of the demands of justice. You would hardly be the first to find that the defence of a mother's interests can threaten those dues that are owed him by a father. A tyranny is a precarious thing, much lusted after by others – and besides, he is an old man, long since past his prime. Do not, then, give away to others the good things that are your own!' Nevertheless, despite having been tutored by her father in all these various blandishments, Lycophron's only response to her speech was to declare that he would never come to

Corinth so long as he knew that his father was still alive.
She duly reported this back. Now Periander dispatched
a third emissary, declaring that he himself wished to come
to Corcyra, and that Lycophron should come to Corinth
and succeed to the tyranny. To these terms his son con-
sented; and Periander duly made ready to leave for
Corcyra and his son for Corinth. So anxious, however,
were the Corcyrans to stop Periander from coming to
their country, once they had got wind of what was afoot,
that they put the young man to death. It was this that
prompted Periander to take his vengeance on the people
of Corcyra.

[54] The force of Lacedaemonians that came to Samos and
began to put it under siege was a formidable one. They
launched an attack against the city walls, and managed to
scale the tower that stood by the sea, on the outer reaches
of the town, only to be driven back when Polycrates
himself arrived with a large number of reinforcements.
Meanwhile, a sally was launched from the upper tower –
the one which stands on the ridge of the mountain – by the
mercenaries and the Samians themselves; but although
they initially succeeded in holding their own against the
Lacedaemonians, they were soon put to flight and cut
down by their pursuers.

[55] Now, if all the Lacedaemonians who were there
that day had proved the peers of Archias and Lycopas,
then Samos would have been taken. For Archias and

Lycopas were the only ones to join the Samians as they fled back inside the city walls, and because this left the two of them with their line of retreat blocked off, it saw them perish inside the city of Samos. Once, in his native village of Pitana, I met with another Archias, a man who was the son of Samius and the grandson of the original Archias, and who esteemed the Samians the most of any foreigners; and this Archias told me personally that his father was given the name of 'Samius' because his own father had died a hero's death on Samos. The reason that he so respected the Samians, he explained, was because they had buried his grandfather at public expense.

[56] For forty days Samos was put under siege, until the Lacedaemonians, unable to break the deadlock, returned to the Peloponnese. There is a more far-fetched account, according to which Polycrates used the local mint to strike a large quantity of coins in lead, which he then had covered in gold leaf and gave to the Lacedaemonians, who took them and only then set off. This was the first time that the Lacedaemonians, or indeed any Dorians, had ever launched an expedition against Asia.

[57] Once they realized that the Lacedaemonians were ready to abandon them, the Samians who had joined the campaign against Polycrates sailed off to Siphnos. They were in need of funds, and this was the same period in which Siphnos was at the very peak of her prosperity: the people of Siphnos were the richest of all the islanders, thanks to the gold and silver mines on their island.

Indeed, these mines were so productive that a tenth of the revenue generated from them was sufficient to endow a treasury at Delphi which was the match, in terms of wealth, of any other there. Every year, the people of Siphnos would distribute the proceeds from the mines among themselves; and so it was, as they were building the treasury, that they asked the oracle whether their current prosperity would continue indefinitely. The Pythia replied:

'Well, whenever the town-halls on Siphnos turn to white,
And the market white of brow, then will you need someone shrewd
To flag for you a battalion of wood, and a herald of red.'

At the time, both the market-square and the town-hall on Siphnos were clad in Parian marble.

[58] The Siphnians were unable to make any sense of this oracle, either at the time or later when the Samians appeared. The point, however, was that the moment the Samians put in at Siphnos, they sent messengers to the city on board one of their ships – and Samian ships, back in ancient times, were always painted red. It was to this that the Pythia had been alluding when she warned the Siphnians to guard against 'a battalion of wood, and a herald of red'. Sure enough, once the messengers had arrived, demanded a loan of 10 talents from the Siphnians

and been rebuffed, the Samians set themselves to stripping the country bare. The Siphnians, the moment they discovered what was happening, went out to the rescue, but were defeated, with many of them being cut off from their city by the Samians, who extorted 100 talents from them.

[59] From the people of Hermione, the Samians took not money but the island of Hydrea off the Peloponnese, which they then entrusted for safe-keeping to the people of Troezen. They themselves, meanwhile, founded Cydonia in Crete, despite the fact that their original purpose in sailing there had not been to colonize it at all, but rather to drive out the Zacynthians from the island. They remained there for five years and prospered to such effect that all the shrines which exist there now, including the temple of Dictynna, were built by them. In the sixth year, however, the Aeginetans combined with the Cretans to defeat the Samians at sea and reduce them to slavery; the boar-shaped prows which the Samians had on their ships were hacked off by the Aeginetans and presented as offerings to the shrine of Athena in Aegina. This the Aeginetans did because they bore a grudge against the Samians, for in the time when Amphicrates had been king of Samos, the Samians had launched a campaign against the Aeginetans, one which had inflicted great damage (although the Samians too had suffered numerous casualties at the hands of the Aeginetans). The entire episode had stemmed from this.

[60] If I have gone on at some length about the Samians, it is because they were responsible for three construction projects which no other Greeks have ever rivalled. One is a tunnel which leads upwards through a mountain some 150 fathoms high, and has mouths at both ends. The tunnel is 7 stades long, and 8 feet high and wide. Dug out along its entire course there is another channel, 20 cubits deep and 3 feet wide, along which water is channelled through pipes from a great spring and brought to the city. Its architect was a man from Megara: Eupalinus, the son of Naustrophus. If that ranks as the first of the three wonders, then the second is a mole which encloses the harbour from the sea: it reaches down some 20 fathoms at its deepest, and is over 2 stades in length. Third on the list of Samian wonder-works is a temple, the largest known to man. The first architect to work on it was Rhoecus, the son of Phileas, a native of the island. Such is the case for covering the Samians in detail.

[61] Now, as Cambyses, the son of Cyrus, was whiling away his time in Egypt, quite out of his mind, there rose in rebellion against him two brothers, Magians both, one of whom Cambyses had left behind to serve him as the steward of his household. This Magian had been prompted to his coup by the realization that the death of Smerdis had been kept a secret, so that there were very few Persians who actually knew of it, most being under the impression

that Smerdis was still alive. These were the circumstances that had set the Magian plotting, and aiming to get his hands on the kingdom. His brother, whom I mentioned as being his partner in the rebellion, was very similar in appearance to Smerdis, the son of Cyrus, whose own brother, Cambyses, had had him executed. Indeed, not only was this Magian similar in appearance to Smerdis, but he even had the same name, Smerdis. 'I will take care of everything for you,' Patizeithes, the Magian, had managed to convince him; and the man was then led by his brother, and seated upon the royal throne. Once that was done, Patizeithes sent heralds off in all directions, but he made especially sure to send one to Egypt, to announce to the army that they were to take their orders in the future not from Cambyses, but from Smerdis, the son of Cyrus.

[62] Sure enough, this proclamation was delivered by the various heralds, including the one who had been detailed to go to Egypt – although, as things turned out, he found Cambyses and his army in Syria, at Agbatana, where he duly stood up among the soldiers and publicly repeated what he had been told to repeat by the Magian. Hearing what had been said, Cambyses presumed that the herald was telling the truth, and that Prexaspes, the man he had sent to kill Smerdis, had betrayed him by failing to do as instructed. 'Prexaspes,' Cambyses said, fixing him with a glare, 'is this how you carried out the mission I gave you?' 'Master,' Prexaspes answered, 'it is

none of it true. Your brother, Smerdis, cannot possibly have risen in revolt against you. You will never have any trouble, no matter where on the scale of danger, from that particular man. I did precisely as you told me to do, and then I buried him – yes, personally, with my own hands. If it is true that the dead are in revolt, then look for Astyages the Mede to rise against you too. If everything continues as it has always done, however, then there is no need for you to fear any injury in the future from your brother. That is why I think the best policy would be to go after this herald and ask him, under interrogation, who it was sent him with this announcement that we should follow the orders of King Smerdis.'

[63] This advice of Prexaspes struck Cambyses as being very sensible, and so the herald was tracked down straightaway and brought back. On his return, Prexaspes questioned him. 'Now, my man, you say that you have come here as the messenger of Smerdis, the son of Cyrus. Tell us the truth, now, and you can be on your way scot-free. Did your orders come directly from Smerdis, in person, or did they come from some underling?' 'I have never once seen Smerdis, the son of Cyrus,' answered the man, 'not since the day that King Cambyses set off on his invasion of Egypt. It was the Magian, the one appointed by Cambyses to be the steward of his household, who gave me this particular mission – although he did say that the order to deliver the speech I gave you came from Smerdis, the son of Cyrus.' All this, delivered

to Cambyses and Prexaspes, was of course the simple truth. 'Prexaspes,' Cambyses told him, 'I exonerate you of the charge of disobedience. You are a good man, and you did precisely as ordered. But which Persian can it possibly be, then, who has risen in rebellion against me, and usurped the name of Smerdis?' 'My Lord,' Prexaspes answered, 'I think I have worked out what has happened. The rebels are a couple of Magians: Patizeithes, the man you left behind as the steward of your household, and his brother Smerdis.'

[64] And it was then, upon hearing the name of Smerdis, that the truth of what Prexaspes had said, and of his own dream, hit Cambyses: for what had he seen in his sleep, if not someone informing him that Smerdis was sitting upon the royal throne, and that his head was brushing the sky? Cambyses realized now that his killing of his brother had been quite needless; so he wept for Smerdis, and then, brushing away his tears, and in agony at the whole wretched business, leapt onto his horse, fully intending to lead his army as fast as he could on Susa, to attack the Magian. As he leapt onto his horse, however, the tip of his scabbard snapped off, and the naked blade of the dagger struck his thigh, wounding him in the very spot where previously he himself had struck Apis, the god of the Egyptians. The wound, Cambyses sensed, was a mortal one; and so he asked, 'What is the name of this city?' Back came the reply: 'Agbatana.' Now, some time previously, the oracle in Bouto had told Cambyses that

his life would end in Agbatana. He had concluded from this that he would die an old man in the Median Agbatana, the city which served him as the hub of his administration; but the oracle, it turned out, had been alluding to the Syrian Agbatana. And when, in response to his question, Cambyses came to learn the name of the city, such was the trauma of the misfortune that the Magian had brought upon him, and of his wound, that he quite recovered his sanity and fathomed the meaning of the oracle. 'It is here', he declared, 'that Cambyses, the son of Cyrus, is fated to meet his end.'

[65] And that, at the time, was that; but then, some twenty days later, Cambyses sent for the most eminent Persians in his train, and said to them, 'Men of Persia, I am obliged by circumstances to reveal to you the matter which more than any other I had been hoping to keep a secret. While I was in Egypt, I saw something in my sleep – a vision that I wish that I had never seen. I imagined that there came to me from my palace a messenger, who reported to me that Smerdis was sitting upon the royal throne, and that his head was brushing the sky. Nervous that my own brother might seize power from me, I acted speedily – but not sensibly. Indeed, although I can see now that no man has it within himself to turn destiny aside, such was my stupidity that I sent Prexaspes off to Susa to kill Smerdis – a terrible deed. Yet once it had been done, I carried on with my life feeling perfectly secure, nor did it so much as cross my mind that with

Smerdis out of the way some other man might rise against me. On every count, then, I missed the point of what was to happen – with the consequence that I became the killer of my brother, and quite needlessly so, since I have still ended deprived of my kingdom. You see, the Smerdis whose rebellion I was warned about in my dream, by the agency of the heavens, was none other than the Magian. But I have done what I have done – and you must come to terms with the fact that Smerdis, the son of Cyrus, is no longer among you. The men now in power in this, your kingdom, are the Magians: one, the steward whom I left behind to administer my household, and the other his brother, Smerdis. There is one man, more than any other, who should have avenged the disgrace that these Magians have brought on me – and yet he, by a most cruel twist of fate, has met his end at the hands of his nearest kinsman. My next best option, then – my brother no longer being here – is one that I must of necessity take: namely, to command you, men of Persia, to fulfil my dying wishes. I call now as my witnesses the gods of the royal household, and lay upon all of you here, and especially those of you who are Achaemenids, this charge: never to let supremacy pass back to the Medes. Should they obtain it by means of treachery, then by treachery you must take it back; should it be force that brings them their success, then you must recover it through the exercise of brute force. Do that, and I pray that the earth will be fruitful for you, and your women and cattle fecund – for you will be, and will forever be, free men. Should you not regain power, however, nor make any effort to recover it, then I pray that the opposite befalls you – and more, that every man in Persia meets an end such as has overtaken me.' And even as he said this, Cambyses wept for all he had done.

[66] When the Persians saw their king in tears, they all tore the clothes that they had on, and gave themselves over to uninhibited lamentation. Later, when the bone turned gangrenous and the thigh had rotted, the wound fast carried off Cambyses, after a reign that had lasted in all for seven years and five months. He died quite child-less, having fathered neither son nor daughter. Meanwhile, the Persians who had been in attendance on him refused to accept that the Magians could possibly have taken power, for they believed all Cambyses' talk about the death of his brother to have been mere disinformation, fed to them with the aim of embroiling the whole of Persia in a war against Smerdis.